The Pil

Christ

Wild Goose Publications

First published 1997

Wild Goose Publications
Unit 15, Six Harmony Row, Glasgow G51 3BA

Wild Goose Publications is the publishing division of the Iona Community.
Scottish Charity No. SC003794. Limited Company Reg. No SCO96243.

ISBN 0 947988 86 6

Copyright © 1996, Christopher Irvine
All rights reserved. No part of this publication may be reproduced in any form or by any means, including photocopying or any information storage or retrieval system, without written permission from the publisher.

The author has asserted his right under the Copyright, Designs and Patents Act, 1988, to be identified as the Author of this Work.

Front cover 'The Winding Way' and six textual illustrations © 1996, Mari Girling

Distributed in Australia and New Zealand by Willow Connection Pty Ltd, Unit 7A, 3-9 Kenneth Road, Manly Vale NSW 2093.

Permission to reproduce any part of this work in Australia or New Zealand should be sought from Willow Connection.

A catalogue record for this book is available from the British Library.

Printed by The Cromwell Press Ltd, Melksham, Wilts.

Contents

Foreword — 4

A Form of Prayer for Welcoming and Commissioning of Pilgrims — 5

A Vigil Service — 13

Daily Prayer for Pilgrims — 21

> *For Use in the Morning* — 21
> *For Use at Midday* — 25
> *For Use in the Evening* — 29
> *For Use at Night* — 33

A Form of Prayer for Those Embarking on a Journey — 43

A Form of Prayer Before a Crossing of the Sea — 45

Pilgrims' Bible Study — 49

An Outline for a Service of Healing and Reconciliation — 53

Pilgrims' Eucharist — 59

A Selection of Pilgrims' Prayers — 69

Readings for Pilgrims — 75

Hymns and Songs for Pilgrims — 83

Notes and Acknowledgements — 93

Foreword

Pilgrimage has been part of the Christian tradition from earliest times. Certain shrines and holy places attracted devout souls from long distances to offer their prayers in thanksgiving and intercession to God. The scallop-shell emblem of pilgrimage became familiar on the route across the south of France and Spain to the shrine of St James at Compostela. Canterbury, Walsingham, Durham, Iona, St David's, and Clonmacnoise were all great centres of pilgrimage at different times from the early middle ages onwards.

Part of the pattern of a pilgrim's life was the interweaving of conversation, common meals and daily prayer. Chaucer's *Canterbury Tales* demonstrates this tradition with humour and sometimes with pathos. Pilgrims learnt from each other through the exchange of common experience. They learnt more about the Christian way. Elements of the monastic pattern of rhythmic daily prayer became part of the pilgrim's spiritual fare.

This short manual offers you a structure upon which the fabric of a pilgrim's day may be woven. Local prayers combined with a pattern known universally in the Church are gathered here as resonant with one tradition. These forms of prayer, readings and songs, remind us of the image of our entire life as a pilgrimage into the heart of God.

We wish you Godspeed as you set out on the Pilgrims' Way.

Stephen Platten
Dean of Norwich Cathedral

A Form of Prayer for Welcoming and Commissioning of Pilgrims

When all the pilgrims have gathered together they are formally welcomed, presented with individual copies of the gospel, and commissioned to take their part in the mission of God, to step out in faith, bearing the good news of Christ and bringing his word of peace to all they meet along the pilgrims' way.

Welcome

Leader:	The grace of our Lord Jesus Christ, the love of God, and the fellowship of the Holy Spirit be with you all!
All:	**And also with you.**
	Dear friends in Christ, God our Creator is ever reaching out in love to his world, He sent his Son, Jesus Christ, to proclaim in word and deed the coming of God's kingdom; the glorious reign of God in which human lives and communities are ordered by God's loving justice, healed, and given hope for the future.
	In his ministry, Jesus gathered disciples and sent them to extend his welcome and his healing touch to outsiders.

After Christ's resurrection, when the disciples were together at prayer, God sent his Spirit, like the rush of a mighty wind, that they might be empowered to unite people of every language, culture and race in the word of the God of hope and peace.

Today, in and through that same Spirit, we too can be caught up in this movement of God. Christ gathers us, as he gathers people from every background, and in every time and place, to hear his word, and to be strengthened for the journey at his table. That word is to burn in our hearts and place a song on our lips. Our sharing in the breaking of bread is to help us recognise Christ as we continue life's journey, and the sharing of his cup helps us to share the joys and sorrows we meet along the way.

Today we have gathered in order that we might be sent out; to enter into the rhythm of God's mission, and to be caught up in God's loving outreach to our world. We have come together to catch the wind of the Spirit and to be led as pilgrims for Christ.

So, in silence let us pray
for the stirring and strengthening
Spirit of God.

Silence is kept

The Prayers

The following litany, or some other form of intercessory prayer shall be offered. The congregation's response, 'Lord, have mercy' may be said, or sung.

Leader: In peace, let us pray to the Lord, saying, 'Lord, have mercy.'

That as we journey together we may discover our unity in Christ, recognise the diversity of our insights and gifts, and look forward to that day when the whole Church is united in the doing of God's will, let us pray to the Lord.

All: **Lord, have mercy**

That we may recognise and celebrate the grace of God in the places we go to and in the lives of those we meet there, let us pray to the Lord.

Lord, have mercy

That we may take the Gospel of the Lord to heart, and speak the word of Christ to others, let us pray to the Lord.

Lord, have mercy

That the peoples of these islands may know the healing touch of Christ, and seek to live peaceably and justly across the divides of race, class, and background, let us pray to the Lord.

Lord, have mercy

> That a greater sense of our calling to
> participate in the mission of God may
> stir throughout the worldwide Church, and
> that we might grow in our sense of sharing
> the life of Christ with Augustine, Columba,
> and Christians of every age and place, let
> us pray to the Lord.
>
> **Lord, have mercy**

To complete our prayer together, let us pray as our Saviour Christ has taught us:

> **Our Father, who art in heaven,**
> **hallowed be thy name;**
> **thy kingdom come;**
> **thy will be done;**
> **on earth as it is in heaven.**
> **Give us this day our daily bread,**
> **and forgive us our trespasses,**
> **as we forgive those**
> **who trespass against us.**
> **And lead us not into temptation;**
> **but deliver us from evil.**
> **For thine is the kingdom,**
> **the power and the glory,**
> **for ever and ever. Amen.**

We sit for the reading from Scripture

The Word

A reading from Luke, chapter 10, verses 1-11

A space for silent reflection is kept after the reading and concludes with the following responsory:

Responsory:

Leader: The Spirit of the Lord is upon me.

All: **He has anointed me to preach good news to the poor.**

He has sent me to proclaim release to the captives;

The recovering of sight to the blind.

To set at liberty those who are oppressed;

To proclaim the acceptable year of the Lord.

A small candlelight procession leads those bringing the copies of the gospels to the front of the church. During the procession the following hymn is sung:

> Thou whose almighty Word
> Chaos and darkness heard,
> And took their flight;
> Hear us, we humbly pray,
> And where the gospel day
> Sheds not its glorious ray
> Let there be light.
>
> Thou who didst come to bring
> On thy redeeming wing
> Healing and sight,
> Health to the sick in mind,
> Sight to the inly blind,
> O now to all mankind
> Let there be light.
>
> Spirit of truth and love,
> Life-giving, holy Dove,
> Speed forth thy flight;
> Move o'er the waters' face,
> Bearing the lamp of grace,
> And in earth's darkest place
> Let there be light.
>
> Blessed and holy Three,
> Glorious Trinity,
> Wisdom, Love, Might,
> Boundless as ocean's tide,
> Rolling in fullest pride,
> Through the world far and wide
> Let there be light.
>
> (Tune: Moscow. Words: John Marriott)

When the procession has reached the altar steps the following prayer is offered:

> God of all wisdom and power,
> we thank you for the gift of your holy word.
> May it be light to our path,
> a lamp to our feet,
> and lead us along the ways of righteousness,
> now and always. **Amen**.

The following acclamation, drawn from a Celtic prayer, is made as the copies of the gospel of Mark are handed over to be distributed to the pilgrims.

Minister:	The Gospel of the God of Life, to guide and protect you.
All:	**The Gospel of Beloved Christ; the holy Gospel of the Lord**.

*An '**Alleluia**' chant is sung during the distribution of the individual copies of the gospel to each pilgrim.*

Afterwards the pilgrims are asked to hold high their copies of the Gospel.

The Blessing and Commissioning of the Pilgrims

> We praise and bless you, God our Father,
> for sending to us your Son.
> He went about among us doing good.
> He travelled light with nowhere to lay his head.

First published 1997

Wild Goose Publications
Unit 15, Six Harmony Row, Glasgow G51 3BA

Wild Goose Publications is the publishing division of the Iona Community.
Scottish Charity No. SC003794. Limited Company Reg. No SCO96243.

ISBN 0 947988 86 6

Copyright © 1996, Christopher Irvine
All rights reserved. No part of this publication may be reproduced in any form or by any means, including photocopying or any information storage or retrieval system, without written permission from the publisher.

The author has asserted his right under the Copyright, Designs and Patents Act, 1988, to be identified as the Author of this Work.

Front cover 'The Winding Way' and six textual illustrations © 1996, Mari Girling

Distributed in Australia and New Zealand by Willow Connection Pty Ltd, Unit 7A, 3-9 Kenneth Road, Manly Vale NSW 2093.

Permission to reproduce any part of this work in Australia or New Zealand should be sought from Willow Connection.

A catalogue record for this book is available from the British Library.

Printed by The Cromwell Press Ltd, Melksham, Wilts.

Contents

Foreword — 4

A Form of Prayer for Welcoming and Commissioning of Pilgrims — 5

A Vigil Service — 13

Daily Prayer for Pilgrims — 21

- *For Use in the Morning* — 21
- *For Use at Midday* — 25
- *For Use in the Evening* — 29
- *For Use at Night* — 33

A Form of Prayer for Those Embarking on a Journey — 43

A Form of Prayer Before a Crossing of the Sea — 45

Pilgrims' Bible Study — 49

An Outline for a Service of Healing and Reconciliation — 53

Pilgrims' Eucharist — 59

A Selection of Pilgrims' Prayers — 69

Readings for Pilgrims — 75

Hymns and Songs for Pilgrims — 83

Notes and Acknowledgements — 93

Foreword

Pilgrimage has been part of the Christian tradition from earliest times. Certain shrines and holy places attracted devout souls from long distances to offer their prayers in thanksgiving and intercession to God. The scallop-shell emblem of pilgrimage became familiar on the route across the south of France and Spain to the shrine of St James at Compostela. Canterbury, Walsingham, Durham, Iona, St David's, and Clonmacnoise were all great centres of pilgrimage at different times from the early middle ages onwards.

Part of the pattern of a pilgrim's life was the interweaving of conversation, common meals and daily prayer. Chaucer's *Canterbury Tales* demonstrates this tradition with humour and sometimes with pathos. Pilgrims learnt from each other through the exchange of common experience. They learnt more about the Christian way. Elements of the monastic pattern of rhythmic daily prayer became part of the pilgrim's spiritual fare.

This short manual offers you a structure upon which the fabric of a pilgrim's day may be woven. Local prayers combined with a pattern known universally in the Church are gathered here as resonant with one tradition. These forms of prayer, readings and songs, remind us of the image of our entire life as a pilgrimage into the heart of God.

We wish you Godspeed as you set out on the Pilgrims' Way.

Stephen Platten
Dean of Norwich Cathedral

A Form of Prayer for Welcoming and Commissioning of Pilgrims

When all the pilgrims have gathered together they are formally welcomed, presented with individual copies of the gospel, and commissioned to take their part in the mission of God, to step out in faith, bearing the good news of Christ and bringing his word of peace to all they meet along the pilgrims' way.

Welcome

Leader:	The grace of our Lord Jesus Christ, the love of God, and the fellowship of the Holy Spirit be with you all!
All:	**And also with you.**
	Dear friends in Christ, God our Creator is ever reaching out in love to his world, He sent his Son, Jesus Christ, to proclaim in word and deed the coming of God's kingdom; the glorious reign of God in which human lives and communities are ordered by God's loving justice, healed, and given hope for the future.
	In his ministry, Jesus gathered disciples and sent them to extend his welcome and his healing touch to outsiders.

After Christ's resurrection, when the disciples were together at prayer, God sent his Spirit, like the rush of a mighty wind, that they might be empowered to unite people of every language, culture and race in the word of the God of hope and peace.

Today, in and through that same Spirit, we too can be caught up in this movement of God. Christ gathers us, as he gathers people from every background, and in every time and place, to hear his word, and to be strengthened for the journey at his table. That word is to burn in our hearts and place a song on our lips. Our sharing in the breaking of bread is to help us recognise Christ as we continue life's journey, and the sharing of his cup helps us to share the joys and sorrows we meet along the way.

Today we have gathered in order that we might be sent out; to enter into the rhythm of God's mission, and to be caught up in God's loving outreach to our world. We have come together to catch the wind of the Spirit and to be led as pilgrims for Christ.

So, in silence let us pray
for the stirring and strengthening
Spirit of God.

Silence is kept

The Prayers

The following litany, or some other form of intercessory prayer shall be offered. The congregation's response, 'Lord, have mercy' may be said, or sung.

Leader: In peace, let us pray to the Lord, saying, 'Lord, have mercy.'

That as we journey together we may discover our unity in Christ, recognise the diversity of our insights and gifts, and look forward to that day when the whole Church is united in the doing of God's will, let us pray to the Lord.

All: **Lord, have mercy**

That we may recognise and celebrate the grace of God in the places we go to and in the lives of those we meet there, let us pray to the Lord.

Lord, have mercy

That we may take the Gospel of the Lord to heart, and speak the word of Christ to others, let us pray to the Lord.

Lord, have mercy

That the peoples of these islands may know the healing touch of Christ, and seek to live peaceably and justly across the divides of race, class, and background, let us pray to the Lord.

Lord, have mercy

That a greater sense of our calling to
participate in the mission of God may
stir throughout the worldwide Church, and
that we might grow in our sense of sharing
the life of Christ with Augustine, Columba,
and Christians of every age and place, let
us pray to the Lord.

Lord, have mercy

To complete our prayer together, let us pray as our Saviour Christ has taught us:

**Our Father, who art in heaven,
hallowed be thy name;
thy kingdom come;
thy will be done;
on earth as it is in heaven.
Give us this day our daily bread,
and forgive us our trespasses,
as we forgive those
who trespass against us.
And lead us not into temptation;
but deliver us from evil.
For thine is the kingdom,
the power and the glory,
for ever and ever. Amen.**

We sit for the reading from Scripture

The Word

A reading from Luke, chapter 10, verses 1-11

A space for silent reflection is kept after the reading and concludes with the following responsory:

Responsory:

Leader: The Spirit of the Lord is upon me.

All: **He has anointed me to preach good news to the poor.**

He has sent me to proclaim release to the captives;

The recovering of sight to the blind.

To set at liberty those who are oppressed;

To proclaim the acceptable year of the Lord.

A small candlelight procession leads those bringing the copies of the gospels to the front of the church. During the procession the following hymn is sung:

> Thou whose almighty Word
> Chaos and darkness heard,
> And took their flight;
> Hear us, we humbly pray,
> And where the gospel day
> Sheds not its glorious ray
> Let there be light.
>
> Thou who didst come to bring
> On thy redeeming wing
> Healing and sight,
> Health to the sick in mind,
> Sight to the inly blind,
> O now to all mankind
> Let there be light.
>
> Spirit of truth and love,
> Life-giving, holy Dove,
> Speed forth thy flight;
> Move o'er the waters' face,
> Bearing the lamp of grace,
> And in earth's darkest place
> Let there be light.
>
> Blessed and holy Three,
> Glorious Trinity,
> Wisdom, Love, Might,
> Boundless as ocean's tide,
> Rolling in fullest pride,
> Through the world far and wide
> Let there be light.

(Tune: Moscow. Words: John Marriott)

When the procession has reached the altar steps the following prayer is offered:

> God of all wisdom and power,
> we thank you for the gift of your holy word.
> May it be light to our path,
> a lamp to our feet,
> and lead us along the ways of righteousness,
> now and always. **Amen**.

The following acclamation, drawn from a Celtic prayer, is made as the copies of the gospel of Mark are handed over to be distributed to the pilgrims.

Minister:	The Gospel of the God of Life, to guide and protect you.
All:	**The Gospel of Beloved Christ; the holy Gospel of the Lord**.

*An '**Alleluia**' chant is sung during the distribution of the individual copies of the gospel to each pilgrim.*

Afterwards the pilgrims are asked to hold high their copies of the Gospel.

The Blessing and Commissioning of the Pilgrims

> We praise and bless you, God our Father,
> for sending to us your Son.
> He went about among us doing good.
> He travelled light with nowhere to lay his head.

Resolutely he set his face to Jerusalem,
and journeyed there to the centre of conflict
compelled by your costly reconciling love.
Bless, these your pilgrims, and guide
their steps as they seek to walk by faith;
strengthen them by your Spirit, today
and until the time when they reach
their place of resurrection.
We ask this in the name of him
who is the Way,
the Truth, and the Life, our Saviour Jesus
Christ. **Amen**.

The hymn 'We have a Gospel to proclaim', (tune: Fulda), or, 'Forth in the peace of Christ we go.' (Tune: Deo Gratias) *may be sung at this point.*

The Dismissal:

Go in the light and peace of Christ!

Thanks be to God. Alleluia, Alleluia!

A Vigil Service

The pilgrims, holding lanterns and torches, gather outside the main entrance of the church in which the vigil will take place. When the ministers arrive, the following dialogue takes place:

Leader: I was glad when they said to me.
All: **Let us go to the house of the Lord.**

Now our feet are standing
Within your gates, O Jerusalem.

Pray for the peace of Jerusalem:
May they prosper who love you.

The whole assembly enters the church, singing the following hymn:

> Glorious things of thee are spoken,
> Sion, city of our God;
> He whose word cannot be broken
> Formed thee for his own abode:
> On the Rock of Ages founded,
> What can shake thy sure repose?
> With salvation's walls surrounded,
> Thou may'st smile at all thy foes.
>
> See, the streams of living waters,
> Springing from eternal love,
> Well supply thy sons and daughters,
> And all fear of want remove:

Who can faint, while such a river
Ever flows their thirst to assuage?
Grace, which like the Lord the giver,
Never fails from age to age.

Saviour, if of Sion's city
I through grace a member am,
Let the world deride or pity,
I will glory in thy name:
Fading is the worldling's pleasure,
All his boasted pomp and show;
Solid joys and lasting treasure
None but Sion's children know.

(Tune: Austria. Words: John Newton)

The minister faces the congregation and from the centre of the chancel step says:

Leader: The Lord says: 'Rebuild my Church'.
All: **May we, as living stones, be built into a spiritual temple, a holy people, and a royal priesthood.**

A large candle, or lamp stand, is brought in and placed at the centre of the assembly; as it is lit, the following prayer is offered:

Leader: Light and peace in Jesus Christ our Lord.
All: **Thanks be to God.**

Let us give thanks to the Lord our God.
It is right to give him thanks and praise.

All praise and glory be to you,
Sovereign God.
You call us into the light of your presence.
From the rising of the sun to its setting
you desire that in every place, praise

and prayer be offered in your holy name.
We thank you that you gather us in the
name of your Son, and through the Spirit
empower us to be his body in the world.
We bless you for the light of your word;
for Augustine, Columba, and all the saints
who in their own generation have borne
the lamp of grace.
May our prayers and praises
be joined with those
of all the saints in light,
and may we ever reflect
your glory, O blessed trinity of love,
Father, Son, and Holy Spirit. **Amen.**

Hymn:

Happy light of temple glory,
Lamp that marks a holy place,
Splendour of the heav'nly Father,
Shining on each Christian face;
We, the children of his lighting,
Show him to the human race.

Mighty day must fade in twilight,
Earth must turn to face the night;
But our Sun appears the brighter
In his gathered children's sight,
Praising Father, Son and Spirit,
Holy God of threefold light.

Worthy in all times and places
To be hymned with cheerful sound,
Son of God, Lord of the living,
Let the universe resound,
Heaven's light by man reflected
On the dreaming world around.

(Tune: Westminster Abbey.
Words: Hilary Greenwood SSM)

During the final verse of the hymn a small procession, led by two taperers, moves into the centre of the congregation to read the Gospel:

The Gospel: John 3:13-22

After the reading of the Gospel, the congregation sings an 'Alleluia' chant:

An address may be given at this point in the vigil.

Reading of the Prayer of St Teresa of Avila

> Christ has
> No body now on earth but yours;
> No hands but yours;
> No feet but yours;
> Yours are the eyes
> Through which Christ's compassion
> Is to look out to the world;
> Yours are the feet
> With which he is to go about doing good;
> Yours are the hands
> With which he is to bless people now.

Silence for reflection

The Beatitudes

Leader:	Blessed are the poor in spirit:
All:	**For theirs is the kingdom of heaven**

Blessed are those who mourn:
For they shall be comforted

Blessed are the meek.
For they shall inherit the earth

Blessed are those who hunger and thirst for justice:
For they shall be satisfied

Blessed are the merciful:
For they shall receive mercy

Blessed are the pure in heart.
For they shall see God

Blessed are the peacemakers:
For they shall be called the children of God

Blessed are those who are persecuted for righteousness' sake:
For theirs is the kingdom of heaven

The Lord's Prayer

**Our Father in heaven,
hallowed be your name,
your kingdom come,
your will be done,
on earth as in heaven.
Give us today our daily bread.
Forgive us our sins
as we forgive those
who sin against us.
Lead us not into temptation
but deliver us from evil.
For the kingdom, the power,
and the glory are yours
now and for ever. Amen.**

Psalm 40, verses 1-11, and 17-19 (*read by a solo voice*)

> I waited patiently upon the Lord;
> he stooped to me and heard my cry.
>
> He lifted me out of the desolate pit,
> out of the mire and clay;
> he set my feet upon a high cliff
> and made my footing sure.
>
> He put a new song in my mouth,
> a song of praise to our God;
> many shall see and stand in awe
> and put their trust in the Lord.
>
> Happy are they who trust in the Lord!
> they do not resort to evil spirits or turn to
> false gods.
>
> Great things are they that you have done,
> O Lord my God!
> how great your wonders
> and your plans for us!
> there is none who can be compared
> with you.
>
> O that I could make them known
> and tell them!
> but they are more than I can count.
>
> In sacrifice and offering you take no pleasure
> you have given me ears to hear you;
> Burnt offerings and sin-offering
> you have not required,
> And so I said, 'Behold, I come.
>
> 'In the roll of the book it is written
> concerning me:
> "I love to do your will, O my God;
> your law is deep in my heart." '

I proclaimed righteousness
in the great congregation;
behold, I did not restrain my lips;
and that, O Lord, you know.

Your righteousness have I not
hidden in my heart;
I have spoken of your faithfulness
and your deliverance;
I have not concealed your love
and faithfulness
from the great congregation.

Let all who seek you rejoice in you
and be glad;
let those who love your salvation
continually say, 'Great is the Lord!'

Though I am poor and afflicted,
the Lord will have regard for me.

You are my helper and deliverer;
do not tarry, O my God.

Taizé chant: 'Stay with us Lord.'

Stay with us, O Lord Jesus Christ: night will soon fall.
Then stay with us O Lord Jesus Christ: light in our darkness.

After a period of chanting and silent prayer the mood and tempo changes with the singing of the final hymn: 'The Spirit lives to set us free', and the service ends informally as the congregation disperses.

> The Spirit lives to set us free,
> walk, walk in the light.
> He binds us all in unity,
> walk, walk in the light.
> *Walk in the light,*
> *walk in the light,*
> *walk in the light of the Lord.*
>
> Jesus promised life to all,
> walk, walk in the light.
> The dead were wakened by his call,
> walk, walk in the light.
>
> He died in pain on Calvary,
> walk, walk in the light,
> to save the lost like you and me,
> walk, walk in the light.
>
> We know his death was not the end,
> walk, walk in the light.
> He gave his Spirit to be our friend,
> walk, walk in the light.
>
> By Jesus' love our wounds are healed,
> walk, walk in the light.
> The Father's kindness is revealed,
> walk, walk in the light.
>
> The Spirit lives in you and me,
> walk, walk in the light.
> His light will shine for all to see,
> walk, walk in the light.

Daily Prayer for Pilgrims

This form is offered that pilgrims may gather each day, either in the morning, midday, or evening, to pray together.

For use in the morning

O Lord, you open our lips;
And our mouth proclaims your praise.

Blessed are you, Lord our God,
to you be glory and praise for ever!
The sun of righteousness has arisen
and calls us to walk in the light of day.
You led Israel from bondage to freedom,
and invited them to enter the land of promise.
In every place and age you call people
to seek your kingdom,
and to serve you as a royal priesthood.
May we continue to journey in your presence
following in the way of your Son,
with the songs of your reconciling Spirit on our lips,
Father, Son and Holy Spirit.

Blessed be God for ever.

The Morning Psalm. Psalm 63

Refrain: **In your unfailing love, O Lord,***
you lead the people whom you have
redeemed.

(The refrain is said by all after each verse)

O God, you are my God;
eagerly I seek you;
my soul thirsts for you,
my flesh faints for you,
as in a barren and dry land
where there is no water;

Therefore I have gazed upon
your holy place,
that I might behold your power
and your glory.

For your loving kindness
is better than life itself;
my lips shall give you praise.

So will I bless you as long as I live
and lift up my hands in your name.

My soul is content,
as with marrow and fatness,
and my mouth praises you with joyful lips,
when I remember you upon my bed
and meditate on you in the night watches.

For you have been my helper,
and under the shadow of your wings
I will rejoice.
My soul clings to you;
your right hand holds me fast.

Reading (taken from 'Readings for Pilgrims' pages 75-82)

The following response may be used before the reading:

Reader:	Early in the morning I cry out to you, O Lord:
All:	**For in your word is my trust.**

The Reading

At the end the reader may say:

The Word of the Lord.
All: **Thanks be to God**.

Prayer

God of all living, you awaken us
with a mother's love and a father's care,
and call us to live in your presence.
Guide and direct us with your Spirit,
in all that we do and say this day.
With open hearts and lives may we
see all that you may show us,
and respond to your calling voice,
that at the day's ending we may raise
a thanksgiving with gladness in our hearts,
through Jesus Christ, our Lord. **Amen.**

The Blessing

Either: Bless, O God, the places we shall see,
Bless, O God, the way that we shall go;

May the people we meet
be your blessing to us,
and your holy name
be blest in all we say,
and think, and do.

Or: May Christ walk the paths we walk;
May his peace be received by all
who welcome us,
and his blessing remain on the places
through which we pass.

(from 'The protection of Colum Cille'.)

For use at midday

O God, come with your saving help.
And make known your healing presence.

Lord Jesus, you came to share our troubles
and shoulder our burdens.
In the heat of the midday sun
you stretched out your arms on the cross.
Embrace with your love and care
all those whom we have
seen and met along the way.
Strengthen us to bear one another's burdens
and so fulfil the law of Christ.
We ask this through Jesus Christ,
our Lord. **Amen.**

A hymn, or song may be sung.

(See 'Hymns and Songs for Pilgrims', pages 83-92)

Psalms 123 and 125

> To you I lift up my eyes,
> to you enthroned in the heavens.
>
> As the eyes of servants look to the hand
> of their masters,
> and the eyes of a maid to the
> hand of her mistress,
>
> So our eyes look to the Lord our God,
> until he show us his mercy.
>
> Have mercy upon us, O Lord, have mercy,
> for we have had more than enough of
> contempt,
>
> Too much of the scorn of the indolent rich,
> and of the derision of the proud.

The psalm may end with the Gloria:

> **Glory to the Father, and to the Son,
> and to the Holy Spirit:
> as it was in the beginning, is now,
> and shall be for ever. Amen.**
>
> Those who trust in the Lord are like
> Mount Zion,
> which cannot be moved,
> but stands fast for ever.

The hills stand about Jerusalem;
so does the Lord stand round about
his people,
from this time forth for evermore.

The sceptre of the wicked shall not hold sway
over the land allotted to the just,
so that the just shall not put their hands to evil.

Show your goodness, O Lord,
to those who are good
and to those who are true of heart.

As for those who turn aside
to crooked ways,
the Lord will lead them away
with the evildoers;
but peace be upon Israel.

Glory ...

A space for silent reflection may follow the reading of the psalm, ending with the following prayer:

God, the source of our joy,
you gladden our hearts
as we journey towards the heavenly city.
Deepen within us a desire for peace,
a longing to see your justice done;
that sharing a common purpose,
your people may prosper and come
to praise you with the songs of Zion,
Father, Son, and Holy Spirit. **Amen**.

A Reading

(taken from the 'Readings for Pilgrims' pages 75-82)

Prayers around the Cross, or beneath the Pilgrims' Banner.

The Taizé chant: 'Jesus, remember me, when you come into your Kingdom.'

The Prayers may conclude with the following:

Leader: Praised be the God who has poured
the Spirit of his Son into our hearts:
All: **Whereby we cry, 'Abba', 'Father'.**

Leader: So, let us gather up all our prayers in the
words our Saviour Christ gave to us.
All: **Our Father in heaven ...**

The Blessing

May Christ show us the path of life,
**and give us grace to take up our
cross and follow him.**

For use in the evening

*The prayer may begin with the lighting of a candle, which may
be accompanied with these words:*

Leader: You Lord, are the fount of life,
and in your light we see light.

The light and peace of Jesus Christ
be with you all
All: **And also with you.**

Let us give thanks to the Lord our God
**Who is worthy of all thanksgiving
and praise.**

Blessed are you, God our redeemer,
you led your people Israel by a pillar
of flame by night, and a cloud by day.
The light of the risen Christ guides
and protects those you call to follow you.

As we reach the end of our day's journey,
set us free by your word of forgiveness,
refresh us by your grace, and renew our
faith, as we place our hope in you,
the goal and end of our earthly pilgrimage,
Father, Son, and Holy Spirit.

All: **Blessed be God for ever.**

A hymn, or song may be sung

A Reading

(taken from the 'Readings for Pilgrims' pages 75-82)

The following response may be used before the reading:

Reader: Your word, O God, is a lantern to our feet,
All: **And a light upon our path.**

Psalm 42, verses 1-10

As the deer longs for the water-brooks,
so longs my soul for you, O God.

My soul is athirst for God,
athirst for the living God;
when shall I come to appear before
the presence of God?

My tears have been my food
day and night,
while all day long they say to me,
'Where now is your God?'

I pour out my soul when I think
on these things:

how I went with the multitude
and led them into the house of God,

With the voice of praise and thanksgiving,
among those who keep holy-day.

Why are you so full of heaviness,
O my soul?
and why are you so disquieted within me?

Put your trust in God;
for I will yet give thanks to him,
who is the help of my countenance,
and my God.

My soul is heavy within me;
therefore I will remember you
from the land of Jordan,
and from the peak of Mizar
among the heights of Hermon.

One deep calls to another
in the noise of your cataracts;
all your rapids and floods
have gone over me.

The Lord grants his loving-kindness
in the daytime;
in the night season his song is with me,

a prayer to the God of my life.

Glory ...

Prayers around the cross, or pilgrims' banner

We bring votive candles and symbols of the day's journey, our encounters with others and the places we have seen, and lay them before the cross. As we pray we might stand with arms fully extended, and hands raised to heaven, so that our bodies form a cross, a posture often adopted by the Celtic monks.

At the beginning of this time of prayer for others the leader may say:

> Come, Holy Spirit of God, and kindle in
> our hearts the fire of your love.

And all respond by saying:

> **Gentle Spirit, stir within us,**
> **that our thoughts and words**
> **may be acceptable prayers in your sight.**

Prayer

Time to bring our prayers for people, situations and places, freely spoken, or unspoken in the silence of our hearts, before God.

Our prayers for others conclude with the Lord's Prayer:

> **Our Father in heaven ...**

Evening Prayer ends with the following responses:

Leader:	O trinity of love,
	you were with us at the dawn of creation:
All:	**Remain with us to the world's ending.**

> You shaped us in our mother's womb;
> **Call us at our life's ending.**

You have walked with us from the
rising of the sun;
**Guard and protect us in the
darkness of the night.**

For use at night

A form of prayer to be used at the very ending of the day

Introduction	Let us reflect on the day that is ending;
recall our journey this day; remembering
those whom we have met and spoken
with; the difficulties we have encountered;
the suffering and the pain that has
touched us, and let us seek God's mercy,
his compassion and forgiveness.

Silence

Prayer of Confession

Either,	You who guided Noah
across the waters of the flood,
Hear us and help us.

By your holy word you
rescued Jonah from the deep,
Free us and bring us to our journey's end.

You who stretched out your hand
to save the sinking Peter,
Help and restore us.

(Adapted from an opening prayer
in the eighth-century Irish Stowe Missal)

34   *The Pilgrims' Manual*

Or, We stumble and fall,
Lord have mercy
Lord have mercy.

We fail to walk in the path
of your commandments,
Christ have mercy.
Christ have mercy.

We forget that your Spirit
dwells within us,
Lord have mercy.
Lord, have mercy.

The Leader then says

Either, May God above us, God before us,
the God who reigns, heaven's king,
have mercy upon us,
grant peace between us, peace within us,
healing rest, and a good journey's end.
Amen.

(from a late tenth-century Welsh poem)

Or, May almighty God have mercy upon us,
set us free from our sins,
and keep us in eternal life;
Through Jesus Christ, our Lord. **Amen.**

Psalm

Either,

Psalm 139　　　　Lord, you have searched me out
(omitting verses 18-21)　and known me;

My body was not hidden from you,
while I was being made in secret
and woven in the depths of the earth.
Your eyes beheld my limbs,
yet unfinished in the womb;
all of them were written in your book;
they were fashioned day by day,
when as yet there was none of them.

How deep I find your thoughts, O God!
how great is the sum of them!

If I were to count them,
they would be more in number
than the sand;
to count them all,
my life span would need to be like yours.

Search me out, O God,
and know my heart;
try me and know my restless thoughts.

Look well whether there be
any wickedness in me
and lead me in the way that is everlasting.

Glory ...

Or,

Psalm 91

He who dwells in the shelter
of the Most High,
abides under the shadow of the Almighty.

He shall say to the Lord,
'You are my refuge and my stronghold,
my God in whom I put my trust.'

He shall deliver you

from the snare of the hunter
and from the deadly pestilence.

He shall cover you with his pinions,
and you shall find refuge under his wings;
his faithfulness shall be a shield and buckler.

You shall not be afraid of
any terror by night,
nor of the arrow that flies by day;

Of the plague that stalks in the darkness,
nor of the sickness that
lays waste at midday.

A thousand shall fall at your side
and ten thousand at your right hand,
but it will not come near you.

Your eyes have only to behold
to see the reward of the wicked.

Because you have made
the Lord your refuge,
and the Most High your habitation.

There shall no evil happen to you,
neither shall any plague
come near your dwelling.

For he shall give his angels
charge over you,
to keep you in all your ways.
They shall bear you in their hands,
lest you dash your foot against a stone.

You shall tread upon the lion and adder;
you shall trample the young lion
and the serpent
under your feet.

Because he is bound to me in love,
therefore will I deliver him;
I will protect him,
because he knows my name.

He shall call upon me
and I will answer him;
I am with him in trouble,
I will rescue him
and bring him to honour.

With long life will I satisfy him,
and show him my salvation.

Glory ...

Hymn: the following, or some other is sung:

God that madest earth and heaven,
Darkness and light;
Who the day for toil hast given,
For rest the night;
May thine angel-guards defend us,
Slumber sweet thy mercy send us,
Holy dreams and hopes attend us,
This livelong night.

Guard us waking, guard us sleeping
And, when we die
May we in thy mighty keeping
All peaceful lie:
When the last dread call shall wake us,
Do not thou our God forsake us,
But to reign in glory take us
With thee on high.

(Welsh tune: 'Ar hyd y nos'. Words: Vs.1,
Reginald Heber, vs.2, Richard Whately)

Reading

(One of the following)

> The servants of the Lamb shall stand before the throne of God and worship. They shall see his face and his name shall be written on their foreheads. There will be no more night; they will not need the light of a lamp, or the light of the sun, for God will be their light.
>
> (Revelation 22:4-5)
>
> Ruth said to Naomi, 'Do not press me to leave you, for wherever you go, I shall go; wherever you live, I will live. Your people shall be my people, and your God, my God. Wherever you die, I will die and there I will be buried. May the Lord do this for me and more also, for even death shall not come between us.
>
> (Ruth 1:16-17)
>
> At night the angel of the Lord opened the prison doors and let the apostles out and said: 'Go and stand in the temple and speak to the people all the words of Christ's new life.' And when they heard this, they entered the temple at daybreak and taught.
>
> (Acts 5:19-20)
>
> And the Lord said to Paul one night in a vision, 'Do not be afraid, But speak and do not be silent; for I am with you, and no one Shall attack you to harm you; for I have many people in this city.'
>
> (Acts 18:9-10)

A short period for silent reflection

Canticle: The Song of Simeon

The Refrain: **Keep us, O Lord, while waking,
and guard us while sleeping,
that awake we may be with Christ,
and asleep may rest in peace.**

Now, Lord, you let your servant go in peace:
your word has been fulfilled.

My own eyes have seen the salvation
which you have prepared in the sight of every people;

A light to reveal you to the nations
and the glory of your people Israel.

(Luke 2:29-32)

Glory ...

The refrain is repeated after the canticle

Concluding Prayers

Our Father in heaven ...

Watch, dear Lord,
with those who wake and watch,
or weep tonight,
And give your angels charge
over those who sleep.
Tend your sick ones, O Lord Christ;

rest your weary ones;
Bless your dying ones;
sooth your suffering ones;
Shield your joyous ones;
and all for your love's sake.
Amen.

(From St Augustine of Hippo)

Leader: Today we travelled as pilgrims;
when we arrived as strangers,
we were greeted as friends,
and shared food and drink.
As the music of the place rings in our ears,

All: **May the divine trinity guard and keep those who welcomed us and all their loved ones.**

(From a Celtic Rune of Hospitality)

Blessing

In peace we will lie down and sleep;

For you alone, Lord, make us dwell in safety.

As the night-watch looks for the morning,
So do we look for you, O Christ.

O thou, most holy and beloved,
our Companion and our Guide along the way,
our bright morning star; raise us up
with the dawn of each new day,
for your love is new every morning. **Amen.**

A Prayer for Those Embarking on a Journey by Coach or Train

The angel said, 'I shall complete the journey with him. Do not be afraid.'

(Tobit 5:21)

If you are going on pilgrimage to find Christ, you will only find him if you carry him in your heart.

(an Irish monastic saying)

Lord God, you call us to walk in faith,
and accompany us along our way.
Grant skill and watchfulness,
care and courtesy,
to all who drive on road, or rail.
May all who travel together grow
in the friendship and love of Christ.
Bring us safely to our journey's end,
and as we travel as bearers of Christ,
may we also find him whom we seek,
even Jesus Christ, the pioneer
and perfector of our faith. Amen.

44 The Pilgrims' Manual

A Form of Prayer
before a Crossing of the Sea

A Celtic Prayer

> Lord of the wind,
> queller of the storm;
> you make the clouds your chariots,
> and ride the waves of the sea.
> Guide and protect us with your peace;
> may your gentle Spirit be our guide,
> and steer us to our haven.

Some verses from Psalm 107

Refrain: **Give thanks to the Lord, who is good, and whose love endures for ever.**

Some went down to the sea in ships
to trade on the mighty waters.
They beheld the works of the Lord
whose wonders are in the deep.

Give thanks to the Lord, who is good, and whose love endures for ever.

Then the Lord spoke and a stormy wind arose,
which tossed high the waves of the sea.
They mounted up to the heavens and fell back to the depths;
their hearts melted because of their peril.

Give thanks to the Lord, who is good, and whose love endures for ever.

They reeled and staggered like drunkards and were at their wits' end.
Then they cried to the Lord in their trouble, who delivered them from their distress.

Give thanks to the Lord, who is good, and whose love endures for ever.

God stilled the storm to a whisper and quieted the waves of the sea.
Then were they glad because of the calm, and God brought them to the harbour they were bound for.

Give thanks to the Lord, who is good and whose love endures for ever.

Reading   *The Lord of Nature*

Either,   Mark 4:35-41

Jesus said to the disciples, 'Let us cross over to the other side'. And leaving the crowd behind they took him with them, just as he was, in the boat. Other boats crossed the water with him. Then a gale arose, lashing up the waves, which struck the boat, and the water almost swamped the boat. And Jesus was in the stern of the boat, his head on a cushion, in a deep sleep. The disciples roused him and said, 'Teacher, do you not care, we are about to sink!' And he stirred, rebuked the wind and said to the sea: 'Be quiet, be restrained.' And the wind dropped and there

Prayer for a Journey 47

was a great calm. Jesus then said to the disciples, 'Why are you fearful and so lacking in courage? Have you no faith?' And they were gripped with holy awe and said to one another: 'Who then is this that both the wind and the sea obey him?'

(Mark 4:35b-41)

Or,   Psalm 93

You, O Lord, are the Sovereign God;
you have put on splendid apparel,
and girded yourself with strength

The Lord has made the whole world so
sure that it cannot be moved;
Ever since the world began,
your throne has been established;
for you are from everlasting.

The waters have lifted up, O Lord,
the waters have lifted up their voice;
The waters have lifted up their pounding
waves.

Mightier than the sound of many waters,
mightier than the breakers of the sea,
mightier is the Lord who dwells on high.

Prayer

Lord, may your peace reign in our hearts
that we may face the chaos of our world,
and journey safely as we seek your eternal
kingdom of justice and love.

Pilgrims' Bible Study

St Columba set off as a 'pilgrim for Christ' across the dangerous seas and carried with him copies of the scriptures. His biographer describes him as a careful scholar who reflected upon and drank deeply from the words of scripture. Like him, each pilgrim should embark not only on a physical journey, but also a journey of discovery, seeking to enter more fully into the story of Jesus and the accounts of those first 'followers of the Way' who kept alive the words Jesus had spoken, and handed on to others the stories of how God's coming kingdom had touched people's lives through their encounter with Jesus.

Those who are taking part in Pilgrims' Way 1997 will be given a copy of Mark's Gospel, and it is envisaged that during a part of each day the pilgrims will spend some time studying the Gospel, perhaps in small groups, in pairs, or alone in quiet time. Those with whom they are staying might well be invited to join this exercise of careful and prayerful reading. The object of the exercise is not simply to read through the Gospel, cover to cover as we might say, but to spend time, taking a small section of the Jesus story, to reflect upon the words recorded there, to imagine the scene pictured in the narrative, and possibly to identify with a character portrayed in the section being read. It is an exercise requiring both thought and imagination, intellect and feelings. The object is to enter into the scripture as well as allowing its words to enter deeply into the reader. Therefore, the words are to be pondered, ruminated, and reflected on, and not just simply read in the usual way in which we read a book.

The words of scripture often strike us more forcefully when they are heard read aloud. So, if the Gospel is being read each day in a group, the first decision to be made is the section of the narrative which is to be read, and then for the passage to be read aloud around the circle, with each person reading a small section, perhaps even just one verse, until everyone has had a turn at reading and the agreed passage has been read.

Why St Mark's Gospel? St Mark's Gospel has been chosen because one early tradition associates it with Rome, the city from which Augustine was sent by Pope Gregory to England. The Gospel is thought to be the earliest written and is actually the shortest. One of its characteristics is the sense of movement in the story of Jesus, and this makes it especially suitable for use by those who are journeying on pilgrimage. The narrative moves along very briskly, and there are very rapid scene changes as the story of Jesus' ministry in Galilee unfolds. The gospel writer frequently uses the Greek word which is generally translated 'immediately', and so, the reader is led from an account of one encounter to another, from one location to another very quickly. The pace of the narrative slows down considerably at that point in the story when Jesus arrives in Jerusalem, and enters the arena of conflict and mounting hostility. This deliberate change of gear helps and encourages the reader to pause and ponder the mystery of Christ's suffering, and the new covenant, or ordering of relations between God and his people, into which we are drawn as we receive the bread and cup of the Eucharist. Another feature which has attracted attention and puzzled biblical scholars is the abrupt ending of the gospel narrative. Unlike the other Gospels there are no post-resurrection appearances of the risen Christ, but a simple story telling how the three women, Mary Magdalene, Mary the mother of James, and Salome, went to visit the tomb on the first Easter day, but an angel announces that Jesus is not there, and that 'he is going before you to Galilee', and the women scurry home afraid, not knowing what to make of it all. It is not immediately obvious what we are supposed to make of this curious and abrupt ending, but perhaps the point is that those who read this Gospel are to take up the story, to make it their own and complete the story of Christ in the unfolding of their own lives. In this way, we might see the story of each Christian life as another chapter, a continuation of the Gospel. For as we are drawn into the story of Jesus and are touched by God's kingdom, so our own lives will show the risen Christ. The Gospel is both a story and a journey, and in that journey we are always summoned onwards and forwards by the words of the angel: 'he has gone before you'. So we set off seeking Christ, guided by his words, on our earthly pilgrimage, on that journey of a lifetime.

Form of Preparation before Daily Reading and Reflecting upon the Gospel

Leader: Come, Risen Christ,
All: **and let our hearts burn within us as you speak to us along the road**.

Psalmody

verses from Psalm 119

Response: **Lord, to whom shall we go?
You have the words of eternal life.**

Happy are they whose way is blameless,
who walk in the law of the Lord.
Who never do any wrong,
but always walk in his ways. *R.*

With my whole heart I seek you,
let me not stray from your commandments.
With my lips will I recite
all the judgements of your mouth. *R.*

I am a stranger here on earth;

Do not hide your commandment from me.
Make me understand the way of your commandments,
that I may meditate on your marvellous works. *R.*

I have chosen the way of faithfulness,
I have set your judgements before me.
I will run the way of your commandments,
for you have set my heart at liberty. *R.*

Make me go in the path of your commandments,
for that is my desire.
I will walk at liberty,
because I study your commandments. *R.*

Prayer

Lord God, we would not seek you,
if you had not found us in Christ.
In this our earthly pilgrimage,
enlarge our hearts,
enlighten our understanding,
that we may walk the ordinary road of life
in freedom, hope, and joy,
through Jesus Christ, our Lord. Amen.

An Outline for a Service of Healing and Reconciliation

[This service will take place at stopping places along the pilgrims' route, and is especially suitable for St David's, Whitby, Lindisfarne, Whithorn, Belfast and Derry. The intention is that each service will capture and express something of the particular concern, ethos, and Christian history of each place, and hence an 'outline' follows to allow for local input.]

Outline for a Service of Celebration and Reconciliation

'Healing the Land'

Welcome

Call to Worship

Hymn, or Gathering Song

Reading of the Gospel: Luke 9:28-36 (The Transfiguration of Jesus)

A Responsory

Voice 1:	Christ was raised from the dead by the glory of the Father, **That we might walk in newness of life**
Voice 2:	Arise, shine, your light has come! **And the glory of the Lord has risen upon you**
Voice 3:	Those who behold the glory of the Lord are changed into his likeness, From one degree of glory to another
Voice 1:	Christ was raised from the dead by the glory of the Father, **That we might walk in newness of life**

When Jesus ascended the Mount of Transfiguration, he did not leave behind the needs and sorrows of those whom he had met, but bore them in his heart, that they too may be transformed by the glory of God's love. So, we also in worship are caught by the vision of God's glory, and stand, like the prophet Isaiah, before the transforming presence of the holy God.

Thanksgiving

Leader: Let us join our voices to the cry of the whole company of heaven, saying:

Holy, holy, holy is the Lord of hosts, the whole earth is full of his glory

We thank God for this cradle place of faith, where your glory has been shown in holy lives and holy places.

A local person lights a large candle to represent the glory of God. A short account of the holy people and special places associated with the locality is read to the gathering.

Another local person leads a prayer giving thanks for the Christian inheritance of the locality.

Confession

Leader: The apostle Paul declares that we have all sinned and fallen short of the glory of God. Let us lament the sins of our communities, the ways in which we have marred God's image in us and spoilt his good creation, saying:

**We are a people of unclean lips
and we live among
a people of unclean lips.
Holy God,
Holy and Strong,
Holy Immortal One,
Have mercy upon us.**

Voice 1: The Lord says: 'If my people who are called by my name humble themselves, pray, seek my face and turn from their wicked ways, I will hear from heaven, and will forgive their sin and I will heal their land.'

In silence local people bring symbols of the wounds, worries and needs of their communities, and place them around the lighted candle. After a spoken prayer of confession, or a period of shared silence, the symbolic objects may be sprinkled with holy water.

56   *The Pilgrims' Manual*

Healing and Reconciliation 57

The Peace

The Peace may be introduced in these, or similar words:

> We are strangers no longer,
> but fellow pilgrims;
> Seeking first God's kingdom
> of justice and peace.
>
> The peace of the Lord Jesus
> be with you all.
> **And also with you.**

An Address

Hymn, or Pilgrims' Song

Prayer of the People for the People

The following form of intercessions is offered as a model:

> Lord of glory, it is good to be here. You have brought us safely to this place and gathered us in your love. Help us to set our faces steadfastly where you would have us go.
>
> Lord, hear us
> **Lord, graciously hear us**
>
> Lord of the nations, you brought your people into a broad and pleasant land; may we take to heart the stories of this place and hold the lives you have touched and bound with ours.

Lord, hear us
Lord, graciously hear us

Lord of the people, you call us from every language, class and culture. Look with compassion upon our sad divisions; may trust overcome suspicion, hope dispel fear, forgiveness banish all bitterness, and draw us all into your peaceable kingdom.

Lord, hear us.
Lord, graciously hear us.

Lord of mercy, you care for us and love all humankind. Bring your saving help to all who are in need. Strengthen those who suffer, and remove all violence, cruelty and terror from our land.

Lord, hear us.
Lord, graciously hear us.

Lord of the Church, you have given us a rich inheritance in the saints of these Isles. May we be inspired by their example and inflamed by your Spirit, that in our generation we may proclaim the eternal Gospel of your Son, Jesus Christ our Lord, to whom be all praise, glory and majesty, now and until the end of the ages.
Amen.

A Prayer of Commitment

A Final Hymn, followed by a Blessing

Pilgrims' Eucharist

The Greeting

When the people have gathered the president says:

> The grace of our Lord Jesus Christ,
> the love of God,
> And the fellowship of the Holy Spirit
> be with you all.

All say: **And also with you**

A Gathering Song

The Collect

The president invites the congregation to pray; silence is kept for a space, and then the president says the Collect:

> God, our saviour and guide,
> who by your calling, summon us
> to live as pilgrims for Christ.
> Help us to travel light,
> to trust your promises,
> and to follow in the footsteps of the saints;
> through Jesus Christ our Lord,
> who lives and reigns with you
> and the Holy Spirit,
> one God, now and for ever. **Amen.**

For all peoples and nations, that God's purposes for peace may be known throughout the world, let us pray to the Lord.

Lord, have mercy

For the people of this country, this city, (this place), that those in positions of trust and influence may act with integrity and seek the good of all, let us pray to the Lord.

Lord, have mercy

For all those who are in need, sickness, or danger, that they may find help in the day of trouble, and be assured of God's saving presence, let us pray to the Lord.

Lord, have mercy

For those who are caught in the circle of violence, that they may grow in trust, and resolve to seek a peaceable and just future, let us pray to the Lord.

Lord, have mercy

For all who travel by sea, land, or air, that the Lord may bring them safely to their journey's end, let us pray to the Lord.

Lord, have mercy

For ourselves and all who gather in this holy place, that we may truly receive God's word, and with gladness hear the good news of Christ, let us pray to the Lord.

Lord, have mercy

The Gospel Reading

The reader announces the Gospel in these, or similar words:

> Let us stand upright and listen to the holy Gospel of the evangelist, Saint. *N*

All: **Glory to Christ our Saviour!**

At the end the reader says:

> Give thanks for the Gospel of Christ.

All: **Praise to Christ our Lord!**

A sermon, or homily may follow.

[A Creed, or other affirmation of faith]

The Confession

A minister introduces the Confession in these or similar words:

> Assured of his goodness, let us acknowledge our need of God's grace to guide and guard us, confessing our sins and asking that he will extend his mercy to our broken world.

All: **O God, rich in mercy and abounding in love, we have sinned against you, in thought, and word, and deed.**

**We have gone our own way and
failed to follow your commandments.
Your love has called us
and our feet have faltered.
Forgive us our sins and
raise us up that we may
walk humbly with you, our God,
act justly, and show kindness,
through Jesus Christ our Lord. Amen.**

The president says:

>As you repent, God forgives you
>and sets you free.
>Forgive others; forgive yourself,
>and approach your God in peace.
>
>The peace of the Lord be always with you.

All: **And also with you.**

All may exchange a sign of peace

The Ministry of the Sacrament

The gifts of bread and wine for the Eucharist are brought to the holy table.

The president may present the gifts, saying this prayer:

>Blessed are you, King of the Universe,
>you provide bread to sustain us,
>and wine to gladden our hearts.
>As our forebears Abraham and Sarah offered

food and drink to the angels at Mamre, so
may our sharing at this table draw us into
closer communion with you, Father, Son,
and Holy Spirit.

All: **Blessed be God for ever!**

The Eucharistic Prayer

The Lord be with you
And also with you

Lift up your hearts
We lift them up to the Lord

Let us give thanks to the Lord our God
**It is right to give you thanks
and praise**

Father of all living, we praise you for your
vast and varied creation,
for the light of sun, and moon and stars;
for the high mountains and low valleys;
for the sea, the surging waves
and mighty winds;
for water in dry places,
and for the green earth.
We thank you that we can marvel
and delight
in the world around us.
You make us, male and female,
in your image,
and give us breath, thought and speech.
Therefore we raise our voices and join
the company of heaven as we sing your
praise.

**Holy, holy, holy Lord,
God of power and might,
heaven and earth are full of your glory.
Hosanna in the highest.**

Your works proclaim your glory, O Lord.
In every age and from every place
you call a pilgrim people to seek your face.

In the fullness of time you sent your Son,
Jesus Christ.
Journeying through Galilee he called people
to follow his way,
seeking first your justice and peace.
With every step he brought your mercy
and healing love to those along the road,
and at his journey's end stretched out
his arms on a cross to bear our pain
and free us from fear.

On the night he was betrayed,
Jesus took bread;
and when he had given you thanks
he broke it,
and gave it to his disciples, saying,
'Take eat. This is my body given for you.
Do this in remembrance of me.'

After supper, he took the cup,
and again giving you thanks,
he gave it to his disciples, saying,
'Drink this, all of you. This is my blood
of the new covenant, which is shed for you
and for many for the forgiveness of sins.
Do this as often as you drink it,
in remembrance of me.'

Therefore, Lord Christ, we proclaim your
self-offering to the Father
on the cross of Calvary;
we celebrate your glorious resurrection,
and rejoice in the outpouring
of the Holy Spirit.

At our beginning the Spirit formed us
in our mother's womb,
and in our earthly life travels with us.
May the Spirit
rest upon this bread and cup,
that we may be nourished
with Christ's being and life,
sustained as members of his body,
and strengthened in our pilgrimage.

**Come upon us, enlivening Spirit,
invigorate, inspire and guide us.**

So, triune God,
may all who gather at this table
be made one in Christ; know your welcome,
and receive a foretaste
of the heavenly banquet.
Draw your whole Church
throughout the world
into your kingdom, where with Mary,
the mother of the Lord, Ambrose, Martin,
Columba, David, Ninian, Augustine,
Hilda and all the saints,
we may rejoice for ever in your presence,
and worship you, Father, Son,
and Holy Spirit,
in songs of never ending praise:

**Blessing and honour
and glory and power
are yours for ever and ever. Amen.**

Eucharist 67

The Lord's Prayer

The Breaking of Bread

> As the grains of wheat were scattered
> and then harvested to make one loaf

All: **So gather your Church into the unity of your kingdom.**

The Communion

The president invites the congregation to receive communion in these words:

> The gifts of God for the people of God.

All: **Jesus Christ is holy,
Jesus Christ is Lord,
to the glory of God the Father.**

Songs, or chants may be sung during the distribution of communion. Afterwards a period of silent prayer is kept, and then the president invites the congregation to pray together, saying:

> Let us pray

All: Lord God, our redeemer,
**you feed your saints
with the bread of angels
and satisfy their thirst
with the cup of salvation.
May we rise from this table
as bearers of your word,**

**and be sent in the strength
of the Holy Spirit
to make your sovereign will
and purpose known;
through Jesus Christ our Lord. Amen.**

Dismissal

Minister: Go in peace to love and serve the Lord.

All: **In the name of Christ. Amen.**

A Selection Of Pilgrims' Prayers

A Prayer attributed to St Columba

According to his biographer, Columba (521-597) sailed from Ireland with twelve other monk missionaries, and his books of Scripture and hymnody, to the Isle of Iona. It is unknown whether he was expelled or exiled from his own land, but he soon came to represent the archetypal 'pilgrim for Christ'.

> Alone with none but you, my God,
> I journey on my way;
> What need I fear when you are near,
> O Lord of night and day?
> More secure am I within your hand
> Than if a multitude did round me stand.

A Prayer in Honour of St Augustine of Canterbury

Augustine (d.c604) was prior of the monastery of St Andrew on the Celian Hill in Rome when he was chosen by pope Gregory to take the Gospel to the Anglo-Saxons. After a long and difficult journey Augustine and his band of thirty monks landed at Ebbsfleet in 597 and was received cautiously by Ethelbert, king of Kent.

God and Father of all living,
your servant Augustine was sent
to strengthen the faith of the English people:
grant that as he journeyed in the Spirit
to bring the Gospel of Christ to the people,
so may all who hear the good news
be brought to a knowledge of your truth,
and see your beauty in the faces of all;
through Jesus Christ, the image of you,
our invisible God.

A Prayer of the Venerable Bede

Bede (673-735) is a Northumbrian saint and spent most of his life as a scholar monk in his monastery in Jarrow. He wrote a number of commentaries on Scripture, but is best remembered for his 'History of the English Church and People'.

I pray you, good Jesus, that as you have given me the grace
to drink in with joy the word that gives knowledge of you,
so in your goodness you will grant me to come at length
to yourself, the source of all wisdom, and to behold your face for ever.

A Prayer of Ambrose of Milan

Ambrose (339-397) was governor of Milan, in Northern Italy, and was elected bishop by popular acclaim. He came to be a wise and influential teacher and writer, and is remembered today for the hymns attributed to his name.

> Jesus, a look from you can draw us from
> our slumbers,
> and set us firmly on our feet.
> Sin shudders and falters at your glance,
> and guilt dissolves into tears of repentance.
> Shine, then, on our torpid minds and set
> our dormant thoughts astir.
> May we leave sin behind us, and our first action
> be to turn to you in repentant prayer.

A Prayer of Columbanus

Columbanus (543-615) was born in Ireland and travelled widely as a monk missionary carrying the arts of Celtic Christianity into the heart of Europe. He was a poet, an 'exile for Christ' and towards the end of his life founded monasteries at Luxeuil and Bobbio, in Northern Italy.

> I beg you, most loving Saviour,
> to reveal yourself to us,
> that knowing you we may desire you,
> that desiring you we may love you,
> that loving you we may ever hold you in
> our thought

A Prayer in Honour of St Hilda

Hilda (614-680) was a Northumbrian princess baptised by St Paulinus. She was guided by the Celtic saint, Aidan of Lindisfarne, and founded a joint monastery of monks and nuns at Whitby. Her wisdom was sought by many people of influence, and the Synod called to decide on Celtic or Roman customs was hosted by Hilda in Whitby in 663.

A Prayer in Honour of St Ninian

Ninian (5th century) was a Scottish saint who took the Gospel to the Picts. His name is closely linked with a monastery and its church at Whithorn. He was influenced by St Martin of Tours and may well have made a pilgrimage himself to Tours.

> Eternal God,
> who called Ninian to proclaim
> your glory in Scotland,
> and to preach to the
> people of northern Britain:
> inspire us with your Spirit
> that we may be heralds
> of your kingdom,
> and increase our appreciation
> of the immeasurable riches
> of the everlasting Gospel,
> through Jesus Christ,
> who lives and reigns with you
> and the Holy Spirit,
> one God, now and for ever.

A Prayer in Honour of St David

David (Dewi) was a bishop and monk who died at the turn of the 6th century. He was a monastic reformer and imposed a rigorous ascetical regime on his communities. His influence and reputation as a holy man extended throughout the southern Celtic lands, and today St David's, in Pembrokeshire, continues as a special place of pilgrimage.

> God of the nations,
> we thank you for the holy life and example
> of your servant David, called to shepherd

your people in Wales.
May we, like him, manifest your love,
grow in wisdom, and faithfully preach
the Gospel of our Saviour, Jesus Christ.

Readings for Pilgrims

The Journey of Faith

Genesis 12:1-3

Now the Lord said to Abram, 'Go from your country and your kindred and your father's house to the land that I will show you. I will make of you a great nation, and I will bless you, and make your name great, so that you will be a blessing. I will bless those who bless you, and the one who curses you I will curse; and in you all the families of the earth shall be blessed.'

God Gives Strength for the Journey

1 Kings 19:7-8

The angel of the Lord came a second time, touched Elijah, and said, 'Get up and eat, otherwise the journey will be too much for you.' He got up, and ate and drank; then he went in the strength of that food for forty days and forty nights to Horeb the mount of God.

The Journey of Liberation

Exodus 14:13-25

Moses said to the people, 'Do not be afraid, stand firm, and see the deliverance that the Lord will accomplish for you today; for the Egyptians whom you see today you shall never see again. The Lord will fight for you, and you have only to keep still'. Then the Lord said to Moses, 'Why do you cry out to me? Tell the Israelites to go forward. But you lift up your staff, and stretch out your hand over the sea and divide it, that the Israelites may go into the sea on dry ground. Then I will harden the hearts of the Egyptians so that they will go in after them; and so I will gain glory for myself over Pharaoh and all his army, his chariots, and his chariot drivers.' The angel of God who was going before the Israelites moved and went behind them; and the pillar of cloud moved from in front of them and took its place behind them. It came between the army of Egypt and the people of Israel. And so the cloud was there with the darkness, and it lit up the night; one did not come near the other all night. Then Moses stretched out his hand over the sea. The Lord drove the sea back by a strong east wind all night and turned the sea into dry land, and the waters were divided. The Israelites went into the sea on dry ground, the waters forming a wall for them on their right and on their left. The Egyptians pursued, and went into the sea after them, all of Pharoah's horses, chariots, and chariot drivers. At the morning watch the Lord in the pillar of fire and cloud looked down upon the Egyptian army, and threw the Egyptian army into panic. He clogged their chariot wheels so that they turned with difficulty. The Egyptians said, 'Let us flee from the Israelites, for the Lord is fighting for them against Egypt.'

The Land of Promise

Deuteronomy 8:6-10

Keep the commandments of the Lord your God, by walking in his ways and by fearing him. For the Lord your God is bringing you into a good land, a land with flowing streams, with springs and underground waters welling up in valleys and hills, a land of wheat and barley, of vines and fig trees and pomegranates, a land of olive trees and honey, a land where you may eat bread without scarcity, where you will lack nothing, a land whose stones are iron and from whose hills you may mine copper. You shall eat your fill and bless the Lord your God for the good land that he has given you.

The Creed of a Travelling People

Deuteronomy 26:5-9

'A wandering Aramean was my ancestor; he went down into Egypt and lived there as an alien, few in number, and there he became a great nation, mighty and populous. When the Egyptians treated us harshly and afflicted us, by imposing hard labour on us, we cried to the Lord, the God of our ancestors; the Lord heard our voice and saw our affliction, our toil, and our oppression. The Lord brought us out of Egypt with a mighty hand and an outstretched arm, with a terrifying display of power, and with signs and wonders; and he brought us into this place and gave us this land, a land flowing with milk and honey.'

The Pilgrim's Longing

Isaiah 26:7-9

The way of the righteous is level; O Just One, you make smooth the path of the righteous. In the path of your judgements, O Lord, we wait for you; your name and your renown are the soul's desire. My soul yearns for you in the night, my spirit within me earnestly seeks you. For when your judgements are in the earth, the inhabitants of the world learn righteousness.

The Pilgrim's Search for Wisdom

Wisdom 51:13-15, 20-21

While I was still young, before I went on my travels, I sought wisdom openly in my prayer. Before the temple I asked for her, and I will search for her until the end. From the first blossom to the ripening grape my heart delighted in her; my foot walked on the straight path; from my youth I followed her steps. I directed my soul to her, and in purity I found her. With her I gained understanding from the first; therefore I will never be forsaken. My heart was stirred to seek her: therefore I will praise the Lord with my tongue.

The Way of the Lord

Isaiah 40:3-5

A voice cries out: 'In the wilderness prepare the way of the Lord, make straight in the desert a highway for our God. Every valley shall be lifted up, and every mountain and hill be made low; the uneven ground shall become level, and the rough places a plain. Then the glory of the Lord shall be revealed, and all people shall see it together, for the mouth of the Lord has spoken.'

God's Pilgrim People

Isaiah 43:1-2, 4-6

But now thus says the Lord, he who created you, O Jacob, he who formed you, O Israel: Do not fear, for I have redeemed you; I have called you by name, you are mine. When you pass through the waters, I will be with you; and through the rivers, they shall not overwhelm you; when you walk through fire you shall not be burned, and the flame shall not consume you. Because you are precious in my sight, and honoured, and I love you, I give people in return for you, nations in exchange for your life. Do not fear, for I am with you; I will bring your offspring from the east, and from the west I will gather you; I will say to the north, 'Give them up', and to the south, 'Do not withhold; bring my sons from far away and my daughters from the end of the earth.'

A Journey of Jesus

John 4:3-9

Jesus left Judea and started back to Galilee. But he had to go through Samaria. So he came to a Samaritan city called Sychar, near the plot of ground that Jacob had given to his son Joseph. Jacob's well was there, and Jesus, tired out by his journey, was sitting by the well. It was about noon. A Samaritan woman came to draw water, and Jesus said to her, 'Give me a drink'. (His disciples had gone to the city to buy food.) The Samaritan woman said to him, 'How is it that you, a Jew, ask a drink of me, a woman of Samaria?' (Jews do not share things in common with Samaritans.)

Christ the Way of Life

John 14:4-7

Jesus said, 'You know the way to the place where I am going.' Thomas, one of the disciples, said to him, 'Lord, we do not know where you are going. How can we know the way?' Jesus said to him, 'I am the way, and the truth, and the life. No one comes to the Father except through me. If you know me, you will know my Father also. From now on you do know him and have seen him.'

Following the Way of Christ

Luke 9:57-62

As they were going along the road, someone said to Jesus, 'I will follow you wherever you go.' And Jesus said to him, 'Foxes have holes, and birds of the air have nests; but the Son of Man has nowhere to lay his head.' To another Jesus said, 'Follow me.' But he said, 'Lord, first let me go and bury my father.' But Jesus said to him, 'Let the dead bury their own dead; but as for you, go and proclaim the Kingdom of God.' Another said, 'I will follow you Lord; but let me first say farewell to those at my home.' Jesus said to him, 'No one who puts a hand to the plough and looks back is fit for the Kingdom of God.'

Healing on the Way

Luke17: 11-19

On the way to Jerusalem Jesus was going through the region between Samaria and Galilee. As he entered a village, ten lepers approached him. Keeping their distance, they called out, saying, 'Jesus, Master, have mercy on us!' When he saw them, he said to them, 'Go and show yourselves to the priests.' And as they went, they were made clean. Then one of them, when he saw that he was healed turned back praising God with a loud voice. He prostrated himself at Jesus' feet and thanked him. And he was a Samaritan. Then Jesus asked, 'Were not ten made clean? But the other nine, where are they? Was none of them found to return and give praise to God except this foreigner?' Then he said to him, 'Get up and go on your way; your faith has made you well.'

The Journey of Paul and his companions

Acts 16:6-12

They went through the region of Phrygia and Galatia, having been forbidden by the Holy Spirit to speak the word in Asia. When they had come opposite Mysia, they attempted to go into Bithynia, but the Spirit of Jesus did not allow them; so, passing by Mysia, they went down to Troas. During the night Paul had a vision: there stood a man of Macedonia pleading with him and saying, 'Come over to Macedonia and help us.' When he had seen the vision, we immediately tried to cross over to Macedonia, being convinced that God had called us to proclaim the good news to them.

God's Sojourners and Pilgrims

Hebrews 11:8-16

By faith Abraham obeyed when he was called to set out for a place that he was to receive as an inheritance; and he set out, not knowing where he was going. By faith he stayed for a time in the land he had been promised, as in a foreign land, living in tents, as did Isaac and Jacob, who were heirs with him of the same promise. For he looked forward to the city that has foundations, whose architect and builder is God. By faith he received power of procreation, even though he was too old — and Sarah herself was barren — because he considered him faithful who had promised. Therefore from one person, and this one as good as dead, descendants were born, 'as many as the stars of heaven and as the innumerable grains of sand by the seashore.' All of these died in faith without having received the promises, but from a distance they saw and greeted them. They confessed that they were strangers and pilgrims on the earth, for people who speak in this way make it clear that they are seeking a homeland. If they had been thinking of the land that they had left behind, they would have had opportunity to return. But as it is, they desire a better country, that is, a heavenly one. Therefore God is not ashamed to be called their God; indeed, he has prepared a city for them.

Ambassadors of Christ

2 Corinthians 5:19-21

In Christ, God was reconciling the world to himself, not counting our trespasses against us, and entrusting to us the message of reconciliation to us. So we are ambassadors for Christ, since God is making his appeal through us; we entreat you on behalf of God, be reconciled to God. For our sake he made him to be sin who knew no sin, so that in him we might become the righteousness of God.

The Journey of Penitence

Luke 15:18-20

The prodigal son said to himself; I will get up and go to my father, and I will say to him, 'Father, I have sinned against heaven and before you; I am no longer worthy to be called your son; treat me like one of your hired hands.' So he set off and went to his father. But while he was still far off, his father saw him and was filled with compassion; he ran and put his arms around him and kissed him.

Hymns and Songs for Pilgrims

1   The Pilgrims' Song

Lord we sing of you upon our way where e-ver we may be as your first disciples in their day went north to Gal-i-lee. To the North with Augustine and Columba, to the North: we shall meet you in Der-ry, ri-sen Lord: we go forth where our is-land saints before went forth: we shall meet you in Der-ry ri-sen Lord.

D.C. senza pausa

Riches I heed not,
nor man's empty praise,
Be thou my inheritance now and always,
Be thou and thou only the first in my heart,
O Sovereign of heaven,
my treasure thou art.

High King of heaven,
thou heaven's bright Sun,
O grant me its joys after vict'ry is won,
Great Heart of my own heart,
whatever befall,
Still be thou my vision, O Ruler of all.

(Tune: Slane; Irish 8th century. Tr. Mary Byrne; versified Eleanor Hull)

3

Christ be with me, Christ within me,
Christ behind me, Christ before me,
Christ beside me, Christ to win me,
Christ to comfort and restore me.

Christ beneath me, Christ above me,
Christ in quiet, Christ in danger,
Christ in hearts of all that love me,
Christ in mouth of friend and stranger.

(Tune: Gartan; from *St Patrick's Breastplate*)

4

Guide me, O thou great Redeemer,	Arglwydd, arwain drwy'r anialwch
Pilgrim through this barren land;	fi, bererin gwael ei wedd;
I am weak, but thou are mighty	nad oes ynof nerth na bywyd,
Hold me with thy powerful hand:	Fel yn gorwedd yn y bedd;
Bread of heaven,	Hollalluog
Feed me till I want no more.	ydyw'r un a'm cwyd i'r lan.

Open now the crystal fountain / Agor y ffynhonnau melys
Whence the healing stream doth flow; / sydd yn tarddu o'r Graig i maes;
Let the fire and cloudy pillar / 'r hyd yr anial mawr canlyned
Lead me all my journey through: / afon iachawdwriaeth gras:
Strong deliverer, / rho im' hynny —
Be thou still my strength and shield. / dim i mi ond dy fwynhau.

When I tread the verge of Jordan, / Pan fwy'n myned trwy' Iorddonen,
Bid my anxious fears subside; / angau creulon yn ei rym,
Death of death, and hell's destruction / aethost trywddi gynt dy hunan,
Land me safe on Canaan's side: / pam yr ofnaf bellach ddim?
Songs of praises / Buddogoliaeth!
I will ever give to thee. / Gwna im' weiddi yn y llif.

(Tune: Cwm Rhondda.
Original words William Williams)

5

To Abraham and Sarah
the call of God was clear:
'Go forth and I will show you
a country rich and fair.
You need not fear the journey,
for I have pledged my word
that you shall be my people
and I will be your God'.

From Abraham and Sarah
arose a pilgrim race,
dependent for their journey
on God's abundant grace;

and in their heart was written
by God this saving word: that
'You shall be my people
and I will be your God.'

We of this generation
on whom God's hand is laid,
can journey to the future
secure and unafraid,
rejoicing in God's goodness
and trusting in his word:
that 'You shall be my people
And I will be your God'.

(Tune: Mountain Christians. Words: Judith Fetter)

6

One more step along the world I go,
One more step along the world I go.
From the old things to the new
Keep me travelling along with you.

Refrain:

And it's from the old I travel to the new.
Keep me travelling along with you.

Round the corners of the world I turn,
More and more about the world I learn.
All the new things that I see
you'll be looking at along with me.
Refrain.

As I travel through the bad and good,
keep me travelling the way I should
Where I see no way to go
you'll be telling me the way, I know.
Refrain.

Give me courage when the world is rough,
Keep me loving though the world is tough.

Leap and sing in all I do,
keep me travelling along with you.
Refrain.

(Tune: Southcott. Words: Sydney Carter)

7

Kum ba yah, my Lord, kum ba yah.
Kum ba yah, my Lord, kum ba yah,
Kum ba yah, my Lord, kum ba yah,
O Lord, kum ba yah.

(Traditional)

8

The wind blows on the mountain side
Where hungry people fed;
The gathered fragments will provide
A single loaf of bread.
So may the Church's members be,
Whatever song they sing,
Drawn into living harmony,
One kingdom for one king.

O secret of the holy food,
The knowledge we are fed,
That we should show our gratitude
By reaching out for bread!
To God the Father let our praise
Join with the holy Son;
For people did in Jesus' days,
And we with them are one.

(Tune: 'House of the Rising Sun'.
Words: Hilary Greenwood SSM, adapted)

9

We are marching in the light of God.
(Siyahamb' ekukhanyen' kwenkhos'.)

(South African traditional. tr. Anders Nyberg)

10

'Moses, I know you're the man',
the Lord says.
'You're going to work out my plan',
the Lord says.
'Lead all the Israelites out of slavery,
and I shall make them a wandering race
called the people of God.'

So every day we're on our way,
for we're a travelling, wandering race;
we're the people of God.

'Don't get too set in your ways',
the Lord says.
'Each step is only a phase',
the Lord says.
'I'll go before you and I shall be a sign
to guide my travelling, wandering race;
you're the people of God.'
'No matter what you may do,'
the Lord says,
'I shall be faithful and true,'
the Lord says.
'My love will strengthen you
as you go along,
for you're my travelling, wandering race;
you're the people of God.'

'Look at the birds of the air,'
the Lord says.
'They fly unhampered by care',
the Lord says.
'You will move easier
if you're travelling light,
for you're a wandering, vagabond race,
you're the people of God.'

'Foxes have places to go,'
the Lord says,
'but I've no home here below',
the Lord says.
'So if you want to be with me all your days,
keep up the moving and travelling on,
you're the people of God.'

(Tune: The People of God. Words: Estelle White)

11

Will you come and follow me
If I but call your name?
Will you go where you don't know
And never be the same?
Will you let my love be shown,
Will you let my love be known,
Will you let my life be grown
In you and you in me?

Will you love the 'you' you hide
If I but call your name?
Will you quell the fear inside
And never be the same?
Will you use the faith you've found
To reshape the world around,
Through my sight and touch and sound
In you and you in me?

Lord, your summons echoes true
When you but call my name.
Let me turn and follow you
And never be the same.
In your company I'll go
Where your love and footsteps show.
Thus I'll move and live and grow
In you and you in me.

(Tune: Kelvingrove (Scottish traditional).
Words: Iona Community)

12 *Solo:* When you walk alone, I'll be there,
I'll be there.
When you walk alone, I'll be there,

All: *For however you travel and the road you follow,*
I'll be there.

When you travel with others, I'll be there,
I'll be there.

When you travel with others, I'll be there.

When you meet someone suff'ring,
I'll bring love,
I'll bring love.

When you meet someone suff'ring,
I'll bring love.

For wherever you travel and the road you follow,
I'll be there.

When you see dereliction, I'll bring hope,
I'll bring hope.

When you see dereliction, I'll bring hope.

Wherever there're people, I'll bring faith,
I'll bring faith.

Wherever there're people, I'll bring faith.

(Tune: Sydney Carter's 'When I needed a neighbour')

13

Who would true valour see
Let them come hither,
In their journey constant be,
Come wind, come weather.
There's no discouragement
Shall make them once relent

Each their avowed intent
To be a pilgrim.

Who so beset them round
With dismal stories,
Do but themselves confound —
Their strength the more is.
No foes shall stay their might,
Though they with giants fight;
Each will make good their right
To be a pilgrim.

Since, Lord, thou dost defend
Us with thy Spirit,
We know we at the end
Shall life inherit.
Then fancies flee away!
I'll fear not what they say,
I'll labour night and day
To be a pilgrim.

(Tune; traditional. Words: from John Bunyan's song in *The Pilgrim's Progress*)

Notes and Acknowledgements

The material contained in *The Pilgrims' Manual* was specifically composed and compiled for the use of those taking part in Pilgrims' Way 1997, an ecumenical venture marking the 1400 anniversaries of the arrival of Augustine of Canterbury and the death of Columba. This pilgrimage from Rome to Derry is essestially a celebration of both the Celtic and Western Christian heritage of these islands. Various stopping places along the pilgrims' routes provide opportunities for gatherings of local Christians, at which both pilgrims and local Christians can share the particular Christian ethos of the place, and bring to God in prayer the contemporary needs and concerns of the locality. In this way, the pilgrimage becomes an important focus and impetus for mission.

The forms of prayer contained here will be a useful resource for all those who plan, or undertake a pilgrimage. In its present form, published by the Iona Community, this volume is offered as a guide to all for whom pilgrimage is a central theme in their view of Christian life and prayer.

Particular thanks are made to Sarelle Reid, managing editor of Wild Goose Publications, for the interest and care which she has shown in this project.

Materials for prayer and forms of worship cannot be written *de novo,* but are shaped and spun from earlier expressions of prayer which resonate with contemporary needs and sensibilities. In this respect, the liturgist is more indebted to others than perhaps any other kind of writer.

The ideas and shape for the *Outline Service for Healing and Reconciliation* were suggested by Russ Parker, the Director of the Acorn Christian Healing Trust. I would like to express my thanks for his interest and support of *Pilgrims' Way*.

The Psalms have a special place in the prayer of Christians, and the version of the Psalms used here is that from the Standard Book of Common Prayer of the Episcopal Church in the USA, in the form used in *Celebrating Common Prayer* (Mowbray), © The Society of Saint Francis 1992, and is used with permission.

The biblical readings are reproduced from *The New Revised Standard Version of the Bible,* Anglicized Edition, copyright © 1989, 1995 by the Division of Christian Education of the National Council of the Churches of Christ in the United States of the America, and are used by permission. All rights reserved.

The *Pilgrims' Song,* by Fr Hilary Greenwood SSM, was commissioned for this volume, and two other compositions of his, *Happy light of temple glory* and *The wind blows on the mountain side,* are used with permission from the Society of the Sacred Mission, St. Antony's Priory, Claypath, Durham.

Two Taizé chants, with music by Jacques Berthier, is used with permission from *Ateliers et Presses de Taizé, 71250 - Taizé Community, France.*

The song *The Summons* is taken from *Heaven Shall Not Wait*, Wild Goose Songs Vol.1 (Wild Goose Publications, 1987) by John L. Bell and Graham Maule, words copyright © 1987 WGRG, Iona Community, Glasgow G51 3UU, Scotland. Reproduced with permission.

The words of Sydney Carter's song *One More Step* are reproduced by permission of Stainer and Bell Ltd.

We are marching in the light of God *(Siyahamb' ekukhanyen' kwenkhos')*, South African traditional. tr. Anders Nyberg, found on *Freedom Is Coming*, © 1990 Wild Goose Publications, Iona Community, Glasgow, Scotland. Reproduced by permission.

The song *Moses, I know you're the man*, words by Estelle White, is copyright © Mayhew McCrimmon, Great Wakering, Essex.

The song *The Spirit lives to set us free*, words by Damian Lundy, is copyright © Kevin Mayhew, Leigh on Sea, Essex.

The prayer in honour of St Hilda of Whitby is used with permission from the Order of the Holy Paraclete, Whitby, Yorkshire.

The words of the song *To Abraham and Sarah*, by Judith Fetter, are reproduced with permission of the author.

Every effort has been made to trace the copyright holders of material reproduced in this book, but apologies are offered for any omissions caused by inadvertence or inability to trace. Such errors, if noted to the publisher, will be put right as soon as possible.

Other material is either traditional or composed by me for and on behalf of the International Steering Committee of *Pilgrims' Way 1997*.

Thanks are also due to colleagues and friends who read and helpfully commented on earlier drafts of this material, especially Dr. Christopher Cocksworth, who read *A Pilgrims' Eucharist,* and Tess Ward for reminding me that the true theologian is 'one who prays aright'. Thanks too to Ruth Irvine for teaching me some basic word processing skills.

Christopher Irvine
Oxford

The Iona Community

The Iona Community is an ecumenical Christian community, founded in 1938 by the late Lord MacLeod of Fuinary (the Rev. George MacLeod DD) and committed to seeking new ways of living the Gospel in today's world. Gathered around the rebuilding of the ancient monastic buildings of Iona Abbey, but with its original inspiration in the poorest areas of Glasgow during the Depression, the Community has sought ever since the 'rebuilding of the common life', bringing together work and worship, prayer and politics, the sacred and the secular in ways that reflect its strongly incarnational theology.

The Community today is a movement of some 200 Members, over 1,400 Associate Members and about 1,600 Friends. The Members — women and men from many backgrounds and denominations, most in Britain, but some overseas — are committed to a rule of daily prayer and Bible reading, sharing and accounting for their use of time and money, regular meeting and action for justice and peace.

The Iona Community maintains three centres on Iona and Mull: Iona Abbey and the MacLeod Centre on Iona, and Camas Adventure Camp on the Ross of Mull. Its base is in Community House, Glasgow, where it also supports work with young people, the Wild Goose Resource and Worship Groups, a bimonthly magazine (*Coracle*) and a publishing house (Wild Goose Publications).

For further information on the Iona Community please contact:

The Iona Community,
Pearce Institute,
840 Govan Road, Glasgow G51 3UU

T. 0141 445 4561; **F.** 0141 445 4295.
e-mail: ionacomm@gla.iona.org.uk

The Pilgrims' Way

1997 marks the twin 1400 anniversary of the death of Saint Columba and the arrival of Saint Augustine who became England's first archbishop.

A Pilgrimage, leaving Rome on 18 May 1997, will be the start of an ecumenical initiative by four nations, England, Ireland, Scotland and Wales, to commemorate and celebrate these early pilgrim Saints, and to pursue their same aims of mission and reconciliation.

Some fifty pilgrims will travel from Rome by foot, coach, train and boat to arrive in Canterbury in time for Saint Augustine's Day on 26 May, and they will be joined by 400 more for various journeys to reach Derry by 9 June, Saint Columba's Day.

There is an opportunity to join the pilgrimage from Canterbury, or to be involved as it passes through your area along main routes which are organized between May - June of 1997: the Eastern route (Canterbury - Lindisfarne - Iona - Ballycastle); the Southern & Welsh Route (Canterbury - Fishguard - Rosslare - Kells - Derry); the Western Route (Canterbury - St Albans - Whithorn - Belfast - Corrymeela). The first group of pilgrims will set off from Rome on Pentecost, 18 May 1997, to spend a week journeying to Canterbury (Rome - Assisi - Taizé - Reims - Canterbury).

By joining the pilgrimage you will be taking your own place in mission history. This is a unique event, and imaginative activities have been planned along each of the routes, with accommodation being provided at all the main staging points.

For more information please contact:

> The Pilgrims' Way 1997 Office
> 12, The Close,
> Norwich
> NR1 4DH
> T. 01603 666900
> F. 1603 766032

This pilgrimage is being supported by all the main Christian churches in England, Ireland, Scotland and Wales, and is being facilitated by The Pilgrims' Way.